FLUTE

PATRIOTIC FAVORITES

Solos and Band Arrangements
Correlated with Essential Elements Band Method

Arranged by
MICHAEL SWEENEY

Welcome to Essential Elements Patriotic Favorites! The arrangements in this versatile book can be used either in a full concert band setting or as solos for individual instruments. The SOLO pages appear at the beginning of the book, followed by the BAND ARRANGEMENT pages. The supplemental CD recording or PIANO ACCOMPANIMENT book may be used as an accompaniment for solo performance.

ISBN 978-0-634-05012-1

HAL•LEONARD®
CORPORATION
7777 W. BLUEMOUND RD. P.O. BOX 13819 MILWAUKEE, WI 53213

00860083

AMERICA, THE BEAUTIFUL

FLUTE
Solo

Words by KATHERINE LEE BATES
Music by SAMUEL A. WARD
Arranged by MICHAEL SWEENEY

FLUTE
Solo

Words by JULIA WARD HOWE
Music by WILLIAM STEFFE
Arranged by MICHAEL SWEENEY

GOD BLESS AMERICA®

FLUTE
Solo

**Words and Music by
IRVING BERLIN**
Arranged by MICHAEL SWEENEY

MY COUNTRY, 'TIS OF THEE
(America)

FLUTE
Solo

Words by SAMUEL FRANCIS SMITH
Music from THESAURUS MUSICUS
Arranged by MICHAEL SWEENEY

THIS IS MY COUNTRY

FLUTE
Solo

Words by DON RAYE
Music by AL JACOBS
Arranged by MICHAEL SWEENEY

00860083

From the Paramount and DreamWorks Motion Picture SAVING PRIVATE RYAN
HYMN TO THE FALLEN

FLUTE
Solo

Music by JOHN WILLIAMS
Arranged by MICHAEL SWEENEY

YANKEE DOODLE/YANKEE DOODLE BOY

FLUTE
Solo

Traditional
Arranged by MICHAEL SWEENEY

From the Motion Picture THE PATRIOT

THE PATRIOT

FLUTE
Solo

Composed by JOHN WILLIAMS
Arranged by MICHAEL SWEENEY

ARMED FORCES SALUTE

FLUTE
Solo

Arranged by MICHAEL SWEENEY

STARS AND STRIPES FOREVER

FLUTE
Solo

By JOHN PHILIP SOUSA
Arranged by MICHAEL SWEENEY

00860083

THE STAR SPANGLED BANNER

FLUTE
Solo

Words by FRANCIS SCOTT KEY
Music by JOHN STAFFORD SMITH
Arranged by MICHAEL SWEENEY

AMERICA, THE BEAUTIFUL

FLUTE
Band Arrangement

Words by KATHERINE LEE BATES
Music by SAMUEL A. WARD
Arranged by MICHAEL SWEENEY

BATTLE HYMN OF THE REPUBLIC

FLUTE
Band Arrangement

Words by JULIA WARD HOWE
Music by WILLIAM STEFFE
Arranged by MICHAEL SWEENEY

GOD BLESS AMERICA®

FLUTE
Band Arrangement

Words and Music by
IRVING BERLIN
Arranged by MICHAEL SWEENEY

00860083

MY COUNTRY, 'TIS OF THEE
(America)

FLUTE
Band Arrangement

Words by SAMUEL FRANCIS SMITH
Music from THESAURUS MUSICUS
Arranged by MICHAEL SWEENEY

THIS IS MY COUNTRY

FLUTE
Band Arrangement

Words by **DON RAYE**
Music by **AL JACOBS**
Arranged by **MICHAEL SWEENEY**

From the Paramount and DreamWorks Motion Picture SAVING PRIVATE RYAN

HYMN TO THE FALLEN

FLUTE
Band Arrangement

Music by JOHN WILLIAMS
Arranged by MICHAEL SWEENEY

YANKEE DOODLE/YANKEE DOODLE BOY

FLUTE
Band Arrangement

Traditional
Arranged by MICHAEL SWEENEY

00860083

From the Motion Picture THE PATRIOT

THE PATRIOT

FLUTE
Band Arrangement

Composed by **JOHN WILLIAMS**
Arranged by **MICHAEL SWEENEY**

00860083

Armed Forces Salute

Flute
Band Arrangement

Arranged by MICHAEL SWEENEY

STARS AND STRIPES FOREVER

FLUTE
Band Arrangement

By JOHN PHILIP SOUSA
Arranged by MICHAEL SWEENEY

THE STAR SPANGLED BANNER

FLUTE
Band Arrangement

Words by FRANCIS SCOTT KEY
Music by JOHN STAFFORD SMITH
Arranged by MICHAEL SWEENEY

MORE
FAVORITES FROM
ESSENTIAL ELEMENTS

These superb collections feature favorite songs that students can play as they progress through their band method books. Each song is arranged to be played by either a full band or by individual soloists, with optional accompaniment on CD.

Each song appears twice in the book, featuring:
- Solo instrument version
- Band arrangement for full band or ensembles
- Pop-style accompaniment CD included with conductor's score
- Accompaniment CD available separately
- Piano accompaniment book that is compatible with recorded backgrounds

Prices:
- Conductor Books $29.99
- Instrument Books $8.99
- Piano Accompaniment Books $12.99
- Accompaniment CDs $12.99

Instrument books for each collection feature separate books for the following: Flute, Oboe, Bassoon, Bb Clarinet, Eb Alto Clarinet, Bb Bass Clarinet, Eb Alto Saxophone, Bb Tenor Saxophone, Eb Baritone Saxophone, Bb Trumpet, F Horn, Trombone, Baritone B.C., Baritone T.C., Tuba, Percussion, and Keyboard Percussion.

BROADWAY FAVORITES
Arranged by Michael Sweeney
Songs include:
Beauty and the Beast
Tomorrow
Cabaret
Edelweiss
Don't Cry for Me Argentina
Get Me to the Church on Time
I Dreamed a Dream
Go Go Go Joseph
Memory
The Phantom of the Opera
Seventy Six Trombones

CHRISTMAS FAVORITES
Arranged by Michael Sweeney
Songs include:
The Christmas Song
  (Chestnuts Roasting on an Open Fire)
Frosty the Snow Man
A Holly Jolly Christmas
Jingle-Bell Rock
Let It Snow! Let It Snow! Let It Snow!
Rockin' Around the Christmas Tree
Rudolph, the Red-Nosed Reindeer.

FILM FAVORITES
Arranged by Michael Sweeney, John Moss and Paul Lavender
Songs include:
The Black Pearl
Fairytale Opening
Mission: Impossible Theme
My Heart Will Go On
Zorro's Theme
Music from Shrek
May It Be
The Medallion Calls
You'll Be in My Heart
The Rainbow Connection
Accidentally in Love
Also Sprach Zarathustra

MOVIE FAVORITES
Arranged by Michael Sweeney
Includes themes from:
An American Tail
Back to the Future
Chariots of Fire
Apollo 13
E.T.
Forrest Gump
Dances with Wolves
Jurassic Park
The Man from Snowy River
Raiders of the Lost Ark
Star Trek

PATRIOTIC FAVORITES
Arranged by Michael Sweeney
Songs include:
America, the Beautiful
Armed Forces Salute
Battle Hymn of the Republic
God Bless America
Hymn to the Fallen
My Country, 'Tis of Thee (America)
The Patriot
The Star Spangled Banner
Stars and Stripes Forever
This Is My Country
Yankee Doodle/Yankee Dookle Boy

THE BEATLES
Arranged by Robert Longfield, Johnnie Vinson and John Moss
Songs include:
And I Love Her
A Hard Day's Night
Yesterday
Get Back
Lady Madonna
Twist and Shout
Hey Jude
Eleanor Rigby
Ticket to Ride
Here, There and Everywhere
I Want to Hold Your Hand

Visit Hal Leonard Online at **www.halleonard.com**

Prices, contents, and availability subject to change without notice.
Some products may not be available outside the U.S.A.